A mother's poignant struggle to comprehend what is ...,
to her daughter. It takes courage to choose to love. Or to grow
up. It takes strength to stand by. It has taken guts to write these
painful words. Words so clear, so frail in their despair and yet so
very calm in the determination to overcome. Words served bite
sized page by page.
Rudolf Krzos, Parent

A generous gift for healthcare professionals, carers, and all who
live with challenges of mental and physical conditions - or simply
with the ups and downs of being human.
Dr Clare Short, Consultant Child and Adolescent Psychiatrist

Bite Sized is a brave and searing account from a mother
navigating her daughter's anorexia, reminding us that eating
disorders do not afflict just individuals but everyone close to
them. Honest and moving, not shying away from how painful it
is, Bite Sized nonetheless offers hope and a side of the story that
needs to be heard.
Katie Green, Author of Lighter Than My Shadow

Fiona's work brings a powerful insight into the impact
that an eating disorder can have on the whole family. Her
compassionate and moving account would help anyone to have
a better understanding of this most challenging illness.
Susan Ringwood, Chief Executive of Beat

Forged by a mother's love, Bite Sized embodies a unique sensory perspective which helps us to grasp the dark complexity of eating disorders in ways no clinical case-study could achieve. Through lived experience and relationship its hard-won wisdom offers hope and is a testament to the resilience of the human spirit.

Catherine Lamont-Robinson, Artist

Compact, compelling and courageous, Bite Sized has the potential to make a real difference. A highly original and powerful piece of writing, it is a brave and honest account of a mother's experience. Anorexia remains surrounded by ignorance and related stigma, which adds significantly to the burden on families. This beautifully written volume will help relatives, friends and many others gain a better understanding of its impact. It should be recommended reading for all healthcare professionals.

Dr Rachel Bryant-Waugh, Great Ormond Street Hospital

Bite Sized speaks to me directly, as I imagine it will to any parent who has witnessed the horror of anorexia; I feel it viscerally. Its meaning extends beyond shared experience, however, and its many layers are bound together with the more universally recognisable ties of love. A book to be shared with anyone who knows what it is to care.

Erica Husain, Parent

Bite Sized

Fiona Hamilton

 Vala

First published in 2014 by Vala Publishing Cooperative

Copyright © Fiona Hamilton 2014

Vala Publishing Cooperative Ltd
8 Gladstone Street, Bristol, BS3 3AY, UK
For further information on Vala publications, see:
www.valapublishers.coop or write to info@valapublishers.coop

Illustrations: Jitka Palmer
Design and typography by Chris Seeley
Typeset in Optima
Printed and bound by CPI Antony Rowe, Chippenham
The paper used is Munken Premium, which is FSC certified.

A CIP catalogue record for this title is available from the British Library.

ISBN 978-1-908363-11-4

Author's Note

Bite Sized is a story from my experience, a personal story. It is not the whole story, but I hope this little book with its few words and plenty of space is enough.

My daughter has given permission for some of her experience to be included. One day she may decide to tell her own story; for now, she is engaged with other creative work. I hope that readers will respond in their own ways and not feel they need to ask for more.

The story is also 'ours'. It is shared by many people. I have met some of them, and I know there are many others all over the world. People affected by eating disorders and by other mental health issues. People navigating the complexity of growing up, or caring for others. Perhaps you will find your own connection with the themes in a different way.

This book comes with a heartfelt thank you to my dear family and friends and to all the many who in different ways have been kind, bold, practical, funny, loving and prepared to learn, change, keep going, not judge, and stay alongside.

Bite Sized is also an offering to many people I don't know, who share in the story in their own ways.

Fiona Hamilton

Foreword
by Philip Gross, author of The Wasting Game

There is a poet's accuracy and tact in these short utterances that sometimes look so slight, so isolated in the white space of the page. The art is in the fact that we might scarcely think (till afterwards) that they are poetry. Any reader whose family has been through a similar experience will recognise the tentative, sometimes faltering, untidy truth of them.

I am one of those readers. Page after page brought back little shocks of memory – yes, I've been there – often in response to tiny details. But I suspect there are few readers who will not catch a resonance somewhere in their circles of family or friends. The dark wing that has brushed them might not be an eating disorder. Many kinds of addiction or obsession seep into the fabric of a family in this way; when this happens, no one is untouched, and all need care. To speak with clarity and sensitivity, in a language so free of the too-available response of guilt or blame, is in itself a kind of care.

This account is not a case history; it is not a family therapy session. This is one person using the disciplines of writing to set down their own journey through the new and suddenly strange landscape into which such an illness pitches the whole family. This writing does not put words into the daughter's and anyone else's mouth ... though

those others might well feel enabled to speak for
themselves through its example.

By speaking sparely, honestly and proffering no pat answers,
Bite Sized offers anyone going though such challenges the
chance to see their own experiences with new clarity –
almost literally to inscribe them in the wide spaces on the
page. At a key moment in the story, a consultant confides
the uncomfortable truth that medical science does not have
the answers to the problem. Rather than being dismayed, the
mother is grateful, is braced by this humility and says
'I trust her more / not less / for telling me / how little we know'.
The way these pieces reach for provisional hope at the end
is all the more moving for its not quite understanding where
it comes from, or why the balance has tipped a little towards
life. Meanwhile, as a working principle, we might share
Fiona Hamilton's humble apprehension here – that 'love'
might be the place to begin.

Bite Sized

One day our daughter got anorexia

Of course, it wasn't that simple

What I remember
is her standing by the window
with her back to me
crying

Was that the beginning?

I remember
she was the only one
who said she didn't want an ice cream
in the half term holiday
a few weeks before

Was that the beginning?

I remember
her infectious giggles
climbing trees right to the top
sucking lemons
singing

That was before the beginning

Maybe the beginning was at primary school
when her best friends stopped being Best
or were only some days
                            - and she never knew which

Maybe it began with girls in the playground
comparing their weight
and one girl puffing up with pride:
                            I'm only four stone

Maybe it began singing solo
in the school concert *I Walk Alone*
applause that left a bitter taste

Maybe it began with a game
of piggyback rides with boys
that depended on lightness

Maybe it began with a lie
We can't lift you
in the dance class

Maybe it began with a morsel
Maybe it began with a bite

Maybe it began with things being too much
Maybe it began with being fed up

Maybe it began with a gut feeling
Maybe it began with something
                              she couldn't stomach

Maybe it began with a gene
Maybe it began long ago

Maybe it began with ashes on the tongue
Maybe it began with a lump in the throat

Maybe it began with ordinary sadness
Maybe it began with wanting something

to be beautifully, perfectly small
or so light it could float away

Our daughter started losing weight

invisibly

then visibly

I watched her eat

I asked her teachers to check she finished her lunch

They said *She is, she's having everything
just like everyone else*

I took her to the doctor

The doctor asked some questions
plotted her weight on her baby chart
did blood tests

The blood test results came through
showing nothing

We went back to the doctor
who did more tests
and sent us home

It was dark
and cold
Christmas was coming

Midwinter:
a phone call in the evening
She's probably got coeliac disease
She'll need an investigation
It'll have to be after the holiday weekend

Time was heavy
Our daughter grew lighter

We got through Saturday and Sunday
but Christmas morning was too much
This can't be right
We carried her in a blanket to A&E

A windowless room
Our daughter on a bed
Tests

Nothing obvious
They sent us home
with build-up drinks

After Christmas she had an operation
to check her intestine

Was this it?
She has coeliac disease
She mustn't eat gluten

They sent us home for the new school term
but she wasn't well enough
to go to school

We brought her meals on a tray
clambering stairs like cumbersome giants
in a shrinking world
Her Dad and I cut up portions
offering bite sized helpings
elfin portions
and sips of water
as if from a thimble
in a desert

Each tiny portion
weighed a ton

It was backbreaking work
like heaving stones
in sweltering midday sun

And then everything stopped

We were back in hospital
hearing the words
She's got anorexia

Maybe that was the beginning
but it felt like the end

anorexia

What an ugly word
anorex rex rex rexia
It wrecks ya, it wrecks ya
anorexia

It means 'loss of appetite'
which is odd
because anorexia
is the hungriest thing in the world

It can eat you alive

And when everything starts again
everything has changed

Our daughter has turned ferocious
she's shouting and swearing
thrashing her arms and legs
with superhuman strength

I swear her eyes have changed
from blue
to cold granite grey

She is refusing to eat or drink anything
not even her saliva
she spits it out
into a plastic cup
over and over
spits it out

There is only one way to keep her alive

Brave girl, says a nurse
threading a tube down her nose

The tube is attached to a machine
that beeps and whirrs
pumping creamy liquid
into her stomach

I dab some from the bottle
onto my tongue

Our daughter gazes at the digital numbers
to calculate how much they are giving her
it has become vital for her to know
it's the most important thing in her world

She keeps trying to pull the tube out
and pinch it closed

The pump is not going to work
so they abandon it
and pour the liquid down the tube
holding it up high to make use of gravity

The young nurse looks miserable
holding the plastic umbilicus
tethering her to my child

I wonder what she thinks of me
as I watch her struggle
to feed my child

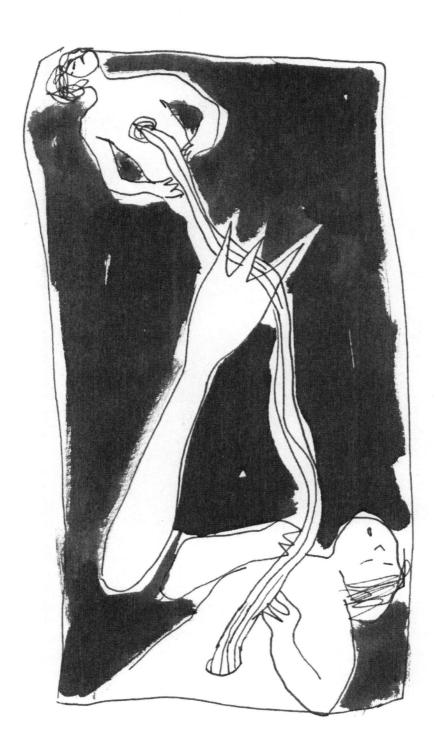

Doctors come and go
asking questions
writing things down

Piles of magazines on the ward
scream headlines
about size zero celebrities
and clever ways to get rid of the kilos

Ballooning celebrities
Skinny celebrities

Lose a stone a month!
How I got back into shape super-quick
after my baby

My baby undernourished
My baby starving
My baby I can't feed

Who else feels like me?

Early mornings dash to the hospital
regular as clockwork
in the cold dark
polite greetings
strangers watching over her
sleeping under a too-thin
hospital blanket
endless grey days
timetabled feeds
meals reduced to sickly liquids
poured through tubes
timed by the clock
measured out in mls

Voices in my head:

This doesn't happen
to babies whose mothers

look after them well
and feed them

it doesn't happen to babies
with mothers who love them

this doesn't happen
it says in the books

everyone knows
this doesn't happen

everyone knows
so what I did, I didn't

oh, what did you do?
what did you?

what didn't you do?

and what I knew
I don't

and who I am
I am no more

Small acts of kindness
fall like rain in the desert

One nurse plays tunes on an accordion
Another brings a book of origami birds

Another lets our daughter try on his boots
which are far too big

Look! we say
You're small and they are big
You're small and they are big
Look!

But it isn't about seeing
It's about believing

and anorexia has taken her beliefs
and twisted them inside out

Minutes
and hours
and days
and weeks
and months
in hospital

Children with broken legs
Children who take their medicine
Children who arrive in wheelchairs
Children who smile at nurses
Children who get better
Children who come
Children who go

Our daughter stays
She shouts and swears at the nurses
She doesn't want their help
She doesn't want their medicine
She doesn't want build-up drinks
She doesn't, doesn't, doesn't

The doctor tells us
*Your daughter has to go to a specialist unit
in a hospital 120 miles away*

I can't compute this
They are going to put 120 miles between us
They say I have to help her
but they are putting all those miles between us

At the far-away hospital
we are invited to a white-walled room

They ask us to draw a family tree
in coloured pens on big sheets of paper
while they watch

We aren't sure why, so we draw in silence

Mum, Dad, son, older daughter
younger daughter
then the names
of aunts and uncles
cousins and second cousins
grandparents, close friends
people alive and dead
drawn on straggly waving branches

Our tree is quite big
but some of the people on it
have no idea what's happening

*This tree could come down in a storm, I think
and it has already been struck by lightning*

Then the meeting is over
Thank you, they say
We'll keep it safe
Someone rolls up our tree
and takes it away

We never see it again

Every few days
we go to see our daughter
My husband and I travel this way and that
passing each other in perpetual motion
leaving our son and younger daughter at home
Sometimes I feel paper thin
stretched out across the miles

On the specialist unit there are

set times
set meals
set amounts
set days
set weighs
set walks
set talks
set places

anorexia likes repetition
it takes the rhythm of life
removes the music
and gives you back a beep
or a whirr
and the clink of cutlery
on an untouched plate

We have to eat family meals
with other parents
and our children who don't want to eat

Come on, have that little bit
Just that bit there
we urge and cajole

Some parents try to chit-chat
while they encourage and urge
Come on, you can do it
You need to have it
Come on

Somewhere between the Mad Hatter's tea party
and a last meal on Death Row
I find my place at the table

Every bite is a grenade of pain
every morsel a heavy boulder
that takes the efforts of several people
to shift from one side of the plate to the other

and if it reaches a mouth
and is swallowed
you can't cheer or whoop
you have to keep your exultation silent
you have to keep quiet
and carry on

Our daughter didn't think in calories
when she arrived at the specialist unit
but now she's the Einstein of calories
They are written on all the meal plans

Eating is a military campaign
that has to be calculated precisely

So is not eating

Mealtime conversations eddy
round and round
before draining away

She asks
Do I have to eat this?
Do I look different?

We don't want to set her back
by saying the wrong thing

We pick our words sparingly
like people on rations
throats parched
guts contorted

Meals stretch out
and contract
like an endless labour
with no birth

In the playground
when I collect our younger daughter from school
I want to join the bright purposeful chatter
with other parents

But even when things improve
it is hard to block out the white noise
of clinking cutlery
on untouched plates
a hundred and twenty miles away

In the night
I wake
fear clutching at my stomach
my head giddy
my thoughts running in loops
my heart thudding

I open our bedroom window
and look into the dark
at the big lime tree
swaying in the wind
breathe
and try to close the vast crater
that has opened up
between me and the ordinary world

Every few days I haul my bike onto the train
pedalling urgently through London streets
feeding on sights and sounds and smells
inviting bricks and tarmac roads and buildings
to imprint themselves in my brain
and be a map of solid things
while tiny white lights
constellations of shock and terror
dance behind my eyes

Each time I visit my daughter
I have to leave her
have to leave her

Goodbye, I say
feeling angry with the nurses
for keeping her

Goodbye, goodbye
sickened by needing
to need them

Goodbye, love you
My reflection in their eyes as I turn to the door
a hideous cartoon of mother, mum – who's she?

a fake, playing along and acting normal
any decent Mum would have
any decent Mum

Goodbye, goodbye
love you, love you
love you, love you

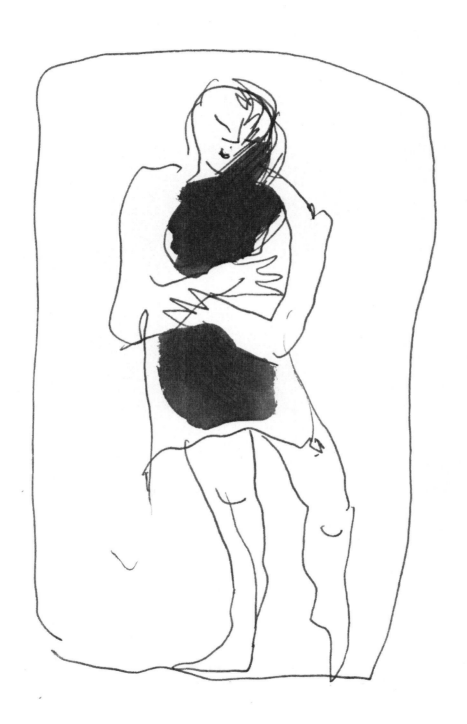

There is a boy on the unit
who has the same dark granite gaze
as our daughter

He has drawn a beautiful swan
in pencil on white paper
which they have framed on the stairway

I see it on the way up
and I see it on the way down

Every few weeks there is a meeting
Hospital staff sit in a circle
with papers in their hands
and we sit, feeling small

Their reports are dry as toast
laden with meal plans and routines
and minutes and hours and calories
and numbers and amounts
and things that are wrong
portions that have been missed
weights
dates

It sounds like somebody else's girl
a girl we don't know
there is nothing about how she climbs trees
to the very top
giggles infectiously
sucks lemons
or sings
but they sound so convinced
we nearly believe them

Half way through the meeting
someone fetches her
and she appears at the door
an elfin creature in a world of giants

No-one mentions the forest of family trees
the desert of white noise
the child whose eyes change colour
from blue to cold granite grey

Our guides are in the dark too

For this is dancing on the edge
and who can say they understand the brain
or the mind?

Who can say they know where the beginning is
or where the end?

Who can say where mind meets body
and how they dance together?

This is dancing on the edge
and who can describe
the movement of a thought?

Is it a wave, or a river?
Is it fibre optic or digital?
How can anyone describe the birth of a feeling?

Mappers of the brain's intricate pathways
are just setting out
into uncharted territory
with a backpack
and pencil and paper
in shorts and big heavy boots

The multi-coloured rainbows of an MRI
promise gold
but cannot tell us where the mind begins
or why some pathways lead helter skelter
into the dark forest

and anyway who cares
when half the world is starving
and right here in front of you
this child has plenty but won't eat?

I think of my daughter as an honest person
but anorexia lies
it's a masterful liar

It lies to you in the mirror
makes a reflection a distortion
twisting everything from true

When you're thin
it magnifies you
to monster proportions

You can be fading away
and it makes you see a giant
looming back at you

It teaches you not to trust anything
except what it shows you
- very convincing lies
with perennial cheerleaders

Ballooning celebrities
Skinny celebrities
Lose a stone a month!
How I got back into shape super-quick
after my baby

Innocent playground games
star-jumps
cartwheels
skipping
turn into instruments of death

Frenetic exercising
calorie burning
sit-ups counted
running on the spot counted
star-jumps counted
calories counted

counting counting counting counting
counting down to zero

Our daughter starts checking
the circumference of her wrists and thighs
over and over
over and over

The more she checks
the less she is sure
It's like an itch
getting stronger and stronger

They have tried to make the unit homely
with sofas, TV, bedrooms, kitchen
but we are utterly lost

Parents wandering helplessly
in a looking-glass world
where our children trade tricks
so they won't have to eat as much next time

Lighter, they want to appear heavier
it's all topsy turvy
drinking water out of hot water bottles
hiding jewellery, pebbles, batteries
in upturned hems, armpits, anywhere

We are the innocents
cumbersome ignorant idiots
and they are the wily magicians

I dream of mirrors
a looking glass world
of opposites

The pull of my daughter's feelings
makes me want to be invisible too

She runs repeatedly on the spot
and I am a hamster on a wheel
walking, pedalling, catching trains
repeatedly rushing to her and back

I wake in the night
spiked by fear

I learn the next day
she woke at the same hour

the umbilical torturer
won't let me rest

Being separate from her
and separating from her

is like tearing off skin
like her ripping herself away

from her compulsions
to risk eating again

Who knows if either of us
can do this?

If she won't eat
can I at least feed her appetite for life?

In the specialist unit they keep pets
There used to be a rabbit on the roof, they tell us
but he died

now there are giant snails
the size of clenched fists
living in a huge glass tank
in a jungle of earth and leaves

That's good, we say
allowing ourselves the faint hope
that children feeding giant snails
might become children feeding themselves
or at least that having a pet
will bring our daughter a little joy

When the snails lay eggs
they are collected
and put in the freezer so they can't hatch
in case the whole place fills up
with multiplying snails

One day after visiting time
I am cycling away
with my head crammed to bursting
and the sick feeling in my stomach

I cycle through some red lights
Can't you see the fucking red?
yells a taxi driver

I can see red
but I don't care
I wish he had run me over

The next morning
I find a bench
in a London square
I start thinking
I will sink without trace
I will disappear
It will be a relief

The flowerbed in front of me
is packed with yellow and purple pansies
moving slightly in the breeze

I stare at them for a long time
They are ordinary
and bright
and very real

With effort
I make a pledge

I believe in love

even when
there is only emptiness
and crying into dark lonely tunnels
where I can't find it
however hard I look
I try saying it to myself
I choose to believe in love

Who would think
a crowd of yellow and purple pansies
could bring life and love
to the wastelands of the heart?

Out of the physical
comes the intangible

Out of genes, molecules, neurons
come desire, loathing, hope, love

But does it work the other way round?

Does the intangible
return to physical?

Do desire, loathing, hope, love
shape the geography of genes, molecules,
                                        neurons?

I don't know
It's beyond me

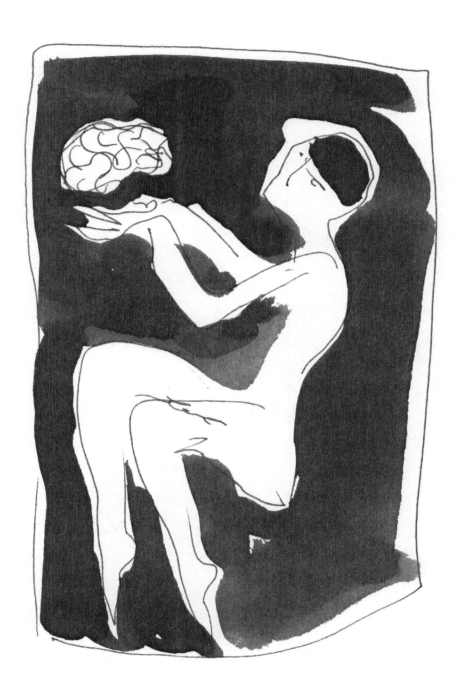

It's beyond her too
the consultant in the hospital
who has written all the books
and knows so much

Even if we could see every little neuron
on an MRI scan, she says
we still wouldn't know how to cure your daughter

I am not upset by her honesty
I am happy with her humility
and her kindness

She isn't doing what anorexia does
she isn't hiding
she isn't lying

I trust her more
not less
for telling me
how little we know

When you don't have answers
and you don't have tools
and you don't have a cure
and you don't have research grants
from pharmaceutical companies
and you don't have a popular cause
that the public will give generously to
when you are with children
who are choosing not to eat
and your guts are churned at the very thought
and you can barely stomach it
and it is easier to turn away
it is hard to hope
it is hard to trust
and to believe there's a way through

Anorexia rears up like a many-headed monster
Each time one head is cut off
another grows in its place

You're in for the long haul
they say
It's a marathon not a sprint

It's several marathons
in a pair of lead boots
that are far too big
without a following wind
in sweltering heat

My friend makes me keep
a tally of 'brownie points'

She texts me every week
What's your brownie point score?

I get brownie points for looking after myself
a good cuppa, a swim, rest, a stroll in the woods,
                                        seeing friends

Someone needed to tell me over and over
that by caring for myself
I am caring for my daughter

I would never have believed them
before it all began
whenever that was

I don't know where the beginning was
or what the ending will be

But I know our daughter is alive and her sparkle...

she sings
makes things out of colourful materials
and her laugh is infectious

She could climb a tree right to the top
but she has to take things steady
because anorexia keeps promising
to show her the perfect self
behind the self she sees

and anorexia keeps threatening
and bribing
and promising
to give her perfection in return for starvation
to show her the way to be light as air
and free from ordinary sadness
and how to take off the heavy boots and float

but anorexia wrecks ya
and is lying
and I think she knows

When anorexia gets your child
it's hard to take your own mirror
out of your pocket
hold it up with conviction
and meet anorexia with its opposites:

its meanness
with abundance

its despair
with hope

its po-faced self-satisfaction
with humour

its isolation
with sociability and team-work

its rigid monotony
with a dance of life

its ruinous destructiveness
with imperfect
ordinary
everyday
irrational
rational
passionate
tender
gentle
firm
strong
yielding
love

But this is the best you can do

Acknowledgements

A huge thank you to everyone who has helped this book into being.

Friends, colleagues and others who read a draft and gave their responses.
Sarah Bird, Jean Boulton, Chris Seeley and all at Vala.
Clare Short for seeing the potential on and beyond the page.
Philip Gross for his kindness and words.
Laila Diallo and Helka Kaski for dancing on the edge.
Jitka Palmer for responding from the depths as human being and as artist.
Alyson Hallett for attention to every little word.
Jonny Glasson and Jamie Lake for a safe haven.
Anna Farthing and Pameli Benham for theatre expertise.
Janie and Chris Grimes for an empowering 'yes' from the beginning.
Tom for living this experience alongside me and showing care and love every step of the way.

About Vala

Vala is an adventure
in community supported publishing.

We are a cooperative
bringing books to the world that explore and celebrate
the human spirit with brave and authentic
ways of thinking and being.

Books that seek to help us find our own meanings
that may lead us in new and unexpected directions.

Vala exists to bring us all into fuller relationship with our
world, ourselves, and each other.

www.valapublishers.coop/bitesized